Fatal Flute and Stick Forms

Wah Lum Kung Fu

Fatal Flute and Stick Forms

by Grandmaster Chan Poi

UNIQUE
PUBLICATIONS

DISCLAIMER

Please note that the publisher of this instructional book is NOT RESPONSIBLE in any manner whatsoever for any injury which may occur by reading and/or following the instructions herein.

It is essential that before following any of the activities, physical or otherwise, herein described, the reader or readers should first consult his or her physician for advice on whether or not the reader or readers should embark on the physical activity described herein. Since the physical activities described herein may be too sophisticated in nature, it is *essential that a physician be consulted.*

Cover Design: Mark Komuro
Book Design: Danilo Silverio

ISBN: 0-86568-059-0
Library of Congress Catalog No.: 84-52680

Unique Publications
4201 Vanowen Place
Burbank, CA 91505

Foreword

This book is invaluable to the serious martial artist. It is the first publication by Sifu Chan Poi, grandmaster of the wah lum tam tui Northern praying mantis style of kung fu, on that system's unique fatal flute form. Further, the wah lum basic stick form, never before presented to the general public, introduces the student to a martial arts weapon exercise which can be traced through verifiable historical sources to the reverend Shaolin temple.

These forms are highly practical for self-defense and exercise. It is not necessary to own complex and archaic Chinese weapons. A short and a long stick are the only equipment required to practice the exercise patterns described in this book. And those interested in improving their self-defense skills will realize that "sticks" are everywhere: Brooms, rulers, shovels, wooden spoons, pool cues, or lengths of pipe are found in practically every environment. Careful and repeated practice of the fatal flute form and basic stick form will gradually give the practitioner an intuitive awareness of the self-defense capabilities of the humble stick.

In this work, Sifu Chan has consented to add a multitude of rich details not often found in martial arts books. The historical and cultural context of the weapons; the preparatory exercises; the fragments of the traditional songs and poems describing the techniques; and the philosophy of weapon use enhance the precise descriptions of the forms to educate and enlighten the reader.

DR. DAVID E. JONES, Ph.D.
ETHNOLOGY

Contents

Grandmaster Lee Kwan Shan

Introduction

History of the Wah Lum Tam Tui Praying Mantis Style

The praying mantis styles of kung fu originated in the Shaolin monastery about 350 years ago, between the Ming and Ching Dynasties.

Wong Long, a student at the Shaolin temple, created the praying mantis style after watching a praying mantis and a cicada fight. He was fascinated by the aggressiveness, speed and strength of the apparently over-matched mantis. No matter how valiantly the cicada fought, the mantis was able to defend and counter-attack, eventually winning the battle. This led to the development of the praying mantis style of kung fu, with its characteristic strong and rapid movements.

It is unclear how the style was passed on through the second and third generations, but the fourth generation successor was Ching Yeung, Abbott of the Wah Lum Monastery of Ping To District in Shantung Province. It was at the Wah Lum Monastery that Grandmaster Lee Kwan Shan studied for ten years to become a fifth generation member of this style. Prior to studying at the monastery, he had travelled the country as an escort, practicing the tam tui system of kung fu, his family style of four generations. In later years, out of respect for the temple, he called his style the wah lum tam tui praying mantis system.

After leaving the Wah Lum Temple, he resumed the life of an escort, conveying goods safely to their destination. His travels took him to Canton, where he accepted many disciples. It was in the village of Sha Cheng, in Po On County of Kwantung Province, that Grandmaster Lee Kwan made Chan Poi, the author of this work, a disciple. I am a sixth generation successor, teaching and spreading Grandmaster Lee's style.

The Qualities
of a Kung Fu Student

The student of kung fu should bring to his study of kung fu humility, respect, and patience. If the student lacks humility, he will be unable to learn. "A filled cup cannot hold more substance." If he has no respect for his teacher, he will neither listen to him nor heed his advice. In the long run, the student will gain nothing. Patience must always be stressed. Any art takes a long time to perfect, and kung fu is no exception. The real secret of kung fu is to "work hard over a long period of time" — the translation of the word *kung-fu*.

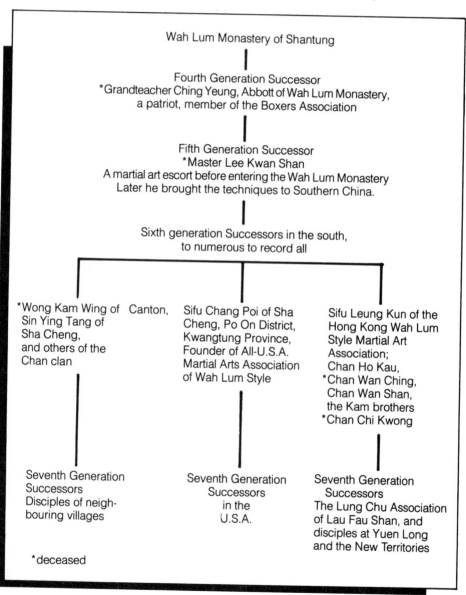

Wah Lum Monastery of Shantung

Fourth Generation Successor
*Grandteacher Ching Yeung, Abbott of Wah Lum Monastery, a patriot, member of the Boxers Association

Fifth Generation Successor
*Master Lee Kwan Shan
A martial art escort before entering the Wah Lum Monastery
Later he brought the techniques to Southern China.

Sixth generation Successors in the south, to numerous to record all

*Wong Kam Wing of Canton, Sin Ying Tang of Sha Cheng, and others of the Chan clan

Sifu Chang Poi of Sha Cheng, Po On District, Kwangtung Province, Founder of All-U.S.A. Martial Arts Association of Wah Lum Style

Sifu Leung Kun of the Hong Kong Wah Lum Style Martial Art Association; Chan Ho Kau, *Chan Wan Ching, Chan Wan Shan, the Kam brothers *Chan Chi Kwong

Seventh Generation Successors Disciples of neighbouring villages

Seventh Generation Successors in the U.S.A.

Seventh Generation Successors The Lung Chu Association of Lau Fau Shan, and disciples at Yuen Long and the New Territories

*deceased

2

To master anything requires total effort in the face of all obstacles. The giant redwood tree is an example. If you walk through a grove of these trees shortly after a rainstorm at sunset, you will experience a beauty that cannot be shared in words. It is only upon quiet reflection that you become aware of the thousands of years these trees have endured fires, storms, and floods to grow to maturity. It is the same sort of perseverance that allows the student to master the martial arts. The road to mastery is filled with goals that initially seem impossible to reach. But those who endure will reap the rewards of kung fu.

The Breath of Nature

When great Nature sighs, we hear winds
Which noiseless in themselves
Awaken voices from other beings,
Blowing on them. From every opening
Loud voices sound. Have you not heard
This rush of tones?

There stands the overhanging wood
On the steep mountain.
Old trees with holes and cracks
Like shouts, maws, and ears,
Like beam sockets, like goblets
Grooves in the wood, hollows full of water.
You hear mooing and roaring, whistling,
Shouts of command, grumblings,
Deep drones, sad flutes.
One call awakens another in dialogue.
Gentle winds sing timidly,
Strong ones blast on without restraint.
Then the wind dies down. The openings
Empty out their last sound.
Have you not observed how all then
Trembles and subsides?

Yu replied: I understand.

The music of the earth sings through a thousand
different holes,
The music of man is made on flutes and instruments,
What makes the music of heaven?

Master Chi said:
Something is blowing on a thousand different holes.
Some power stands behind all this and
Makes the sound die down.
What is the power?

—From The Way of Chuang Tzu

1.
The Fatal Flute

The Flute in Chinese Culture

The flute, a tube through which a tone-producing stream of air is projected, is the most ancient musical instrument known. It is also one of the most widespread, and is found in some form (whistle, panpipe, flageolet) in almost all cultures. However, regardless of its great age and its near universal presence in the world, its origin remains obscure. Probably it was independently invented in a number of places, and was created even before the appearance of modern homo sapiens some 40,000 years ago.

How the first flute was created is a mystery, but some imaginative possiblities can be offered, based on what is known of ancient hunting peoples. All hunting-and-gathering tribes found the marrow of the bone to be a delicacy, and would smash, split, and cut the bone to dig or suck out the marrow. From this daily exercise they could have observed that breath moving through a hollow tube makes an interesting sound. The most complete archeological site revealing the existence of pre-homo sapiens hunters is Chou Kou Tien, a cave system near present-day Peking (Bejing). The remains there date back to 500,000 B.C. and show evidence of this marrow-extracting activity. It is significant that ancient, as well as contemporary, hunters and gatherers typically make flutes and whistles out of bone. Though it is known that hunters and gatherers rarely fought one another, the bone flute could have been used as a weapon of self-defense against predatory animals.

In those parts of the world blessed with an abundance of bamboo, another everyday occurrence might have helped create the first flute. Children everywhere sooner or later discover the pleasant humming sound that can be made by blowing over the top of a narrow-mouthed jar, bottle, or reed. Imagine a group of wandering Asian hunters preparing their camp at days end. They cut bamboo for a temporary shelter and settle in for the night. A warm wind moves in the dark. The varying lengths of the bamboo stalk sections would produce a range of tones as random gusts and breezes played across the open ends. The panpipe comes to mind. Bind together a number of tubes of varying lengths and blow over the top of them. Scales and simple chords can be created.

The panpipe was, in fact, known from the beginning of recorded history in China. A specialist in this area, William Malm, writes:

> In ancient China, the proper tuning of the imperial music was of great importance to the maintenance of earthly and celestial unanimity. Every new emperor required a remeasurement of the pipes used to tune the court orchestra. A band of such pipes, called a hsiao, became part of the orchestra itself. This type of panpipe was eventually disassembled, and each pipe was fitted with five holes so that melodies could be played upon it.

Great works of Chinese art verify the existence of the flute in all strata of society over thousands of years. Drawings exist depicting scenes from the Shang Dynasty (c. 1520-1030 B.C.) in which the five-hole flute is represented. One example shows a young cowherd riding a cow and playing his flute. In the Han Dynasty (202 B.C.-A.D. 220) paintings appear of the "Eight Immortal Drunken Gods," one of which, Han Hsiang-Tzu, is shown with a flute. Also from the Han period, ceramic tiles portray musicians playing flutes for dancers. In the Sung Dynasty (420-479 A.D.), a classic miniature painting reveals children playing flutes. During the Tang Dynasty (618-906 A.D.) artistic endeavors ranging from burial ceramics to paintings depict the use of the flute. Thousands of drawings, paintings, and statuary from the Ming Dynasty (1368-1644 A.D.) into modern times bear witness to the place of the flute in Chinese culture. In addition, Curt Sachs, in his book The History of Musical Instruments, states that the flute is described from the very beginnings of China's literary tradition. The most ancient Chinese flute, the kuan and hsaio, is noted in written accounts dating to the 12th century B.C. (Shang Dynasty).

The flute's relationship to the arts of war appears first in oral traditions from the beginning of the Han Dynasty. One such record describes a military confrontation between the armies of the Han and the Chu on the Black river. Secretary Cheung Leung single-handedly won the battle by two unique acts. He created a large kite in which to ride over the river separating the enemy armies. This is recounted as the first use of the kite in warfare for reconnaissance. Further, while riding his war kite in the night sky and looking down upon his enemy, he played his flute with such beauty that the soldiers of the other side grew homesick and melancholy, and left the battle field without a struggle.

The Tang Dynasty poet, Ts'en Shen, described a similar scene in a poem telling of the feelings of Chinese fighting men at a party held for them in the village of Wine Springs on the Central Asian frontier:

The Grand Protector of Wine Springs,
expert at the sword dance,
Set out the wine in his high hall —
his drums beat in the night.
Just one song on the barbarian pipe rent
our bowels —
We seated visitors gazed at each other, our
tears like rain.

The flute's relationship to the warrior can be seen in another context. From the late Chou Dynasty, Chinese society was divided into four classes. The people of the top rank were called the *shi*. The *Book of Han* states: "The *shi*, the farmer, the craftsman, and the tradesman are the four professions of the people. He who occupies his rank by means of learning is called a *shi*."

Wilson, in *Origin of The Warrior Class*, states that "the *shi* originated in the late Chou Dynasty as the descendents of landed nobility — well-educated and armed." The well-educated man of old China was expected to master a musical instrument along with a variety of other artistic, literary, cultural, and technical abilities. The flute was a common choice of the *shi* warrior/scholar because it was light and portable, and also, perhaps, because of its potential as a weapon of self-defense.

The Fatal Flute: A Philosophy of Use

The flute-as-weapon can be carried easily and inconspicuously. It can also be concealed on the person, and can be used a secret weapon for close-in violent encounters of a defensive nature. Further, the movements of the flute-weapon are similar to the techniques of the iron ribbed fan, the iron ruler (*te chek*), and the dagger, and would be at least familiar to the practitioner of traditional Chinese martial arts.

Flute-weapons are made of jade, bamboo, bronze, iron, and steel. They average between 16 and 24 inches in length. The ideal length would be measured from the tip of the longest finger of the right hand when fully extended to slightly beyond the right elbow. The rationale for this length is found in the ability of the forearm block, strike, or parry to be augmented by a hard ridge — the flute.

From the earliest use of the flute as a weapon, its potential as a projectile launcher has been appreciated. The flute was used to deliver poison darts and powders. It can also house daggers and large pins capable of penetrating vital organs. These uses are considered deplorable by the Wah Lum system and evidence of the corrupt nature of the user.

The sound martial artist sees the flute as a dangerous weapon and respects its potential. The form presented in this book will teach methods of striking and attacking the nerves

A. Bamboo
B. Hardwood
C. Metal

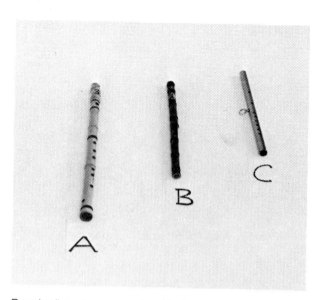

Regular flute size ranges from 14 inches to 18 inches.

and pressure points which can prove fatal. Intelligence, sensitivity, a good heart, and a compassionate nature are required of the martial artist. Otherwise he becomes a mere thug and bully armed with dangerous knowledge.

The qualities of the excellent martial artist have been stated since ancient times. The true martial artist is gentle and humble. They are people who abhor violence, people who seek peace. Remember that the Chinese character for "martial arts" literally reads "stop fighting." It is said that if you study kung fu for one year, you can fight two people. If you study kung fu for three years, you can fight five people; but if you study kung fu for ten years, you will fight no one. The secret to a dignified peace is found in control brought about by serious practice, experience, humane philosophy, and mental, physical, and spiritual development and maturity. Those who believe that the martial arts are primarily intended for fighting simply do not understand the true intent of the methods they practice.

The following are qualities of developed martial artists:
1) They move like the wind;
2) They have the repose of a mountain. They are dignified and awesome;
3) They have the explosive power of a tiger;
4) They have the light, quick footwork of a rabbit;
5) They have the grasping power of an eagle;
6) They are soft and yielding like a snake — flexible and adaptable;
7) They have quickness in the movements of the eyes, the hands, and the body;
8) They have the control, stealth, and lightning attack of a hunting cat;
9) They have a self-knowledge that allows them to judge the level or expertise of another simply by watching him;

10) They know when to fight and when to run away. They match their courage and prowess with intelligence;

11) They are calm and patient;

12) They respect all adversaries with a humble but not submissive attitude.

Finally, it might be noted that from earliest times the flute has held a special place in the East as a philosophical and artistic symbol of man. It is empty and hollow, only coming to life when the human spirit moves in it. Its music purely reflects the nature and character of the one who plays it. The flute's music is the player's breath. This is not a weapon of the tiger nature, nor the dragon, nor the snake; it is a weapon with a powerful human nature. One can interpret or portray the dragon nature in a fighting posture or form, but the flute allows only the human spirit to be projected. As you practice the techniques, exercises, and fatal flute form, consider that in the special way you are playing the flute, your human nature is being revealed to you and to others.

Exercises With The Flute

First Set

1. Both hands grip the ends of the flute, which is then raised to the height of the shoulders. The flute is now horizontal.

2. The right arm then moves inward towards the body, and then up and out, while the left hand turns the other end of the flute downward. The right elbow now points downwards to the wrist of the left arm and the flute is vertical in direction.

3. The twist is then reversed.

4. The two ends of the flute, held by both hands, are then pushed sideways, so that the arms are crossed, and the flute becomes horizontal.

Second Set

1. From the cross-armed holding position (at the end of the first set), the right end of the flute is moved over the head to the back, while keeping the left end low.

2. From the back, the right end of the flute is moved towards the left arm and shoulder.

3. While the left hand keeps the left end of the flute still, the right hand moves the right end of the flute towards the left elbow.

12

4. The right hand keeps moving forward around the left elbow until both arms are again crossed.

Third Set

1. Starting from the position at the end of the second set, the hands move towards the right shoulder until they reach the back of the head.

2. The flute is turned by moving the right hand up and moving the left hand down, while raising the left shoulder and lowering the right shoulder.

3. The left hand moves the left end of the flute towards the back of the left shoulder.

4. The left hand moves to the back of the neck, while the right hand is placed at the back of the waist, so that the hands are one above the other. The flute is now being held in a vertical position.

5. The left arm moves first over the head and then towards the right shoulder while the right hand stays at the back of the waist.

6. Both hands move to the right so that the flute slips along the right arm towards the right elbow until it comes up from under the right elbow.

Basic Methods of Manipulating The Flute

A strong grip and flexible wrists are necessary to manipulate the fatal flute correctly and efficiently. A good exercise for the development of strong gripping power is to expand the fingers widely and then contract them quickly and tightly into a fist. This should be done several hundred times in each daily practice session. Of course, flexibility and strength in the wrists will be greatly enhanced simply by practicing the fatal flute form.

The following photographs depict some of the basic grasping and manipulating methods employed with the flute.

Ready (attack) posture

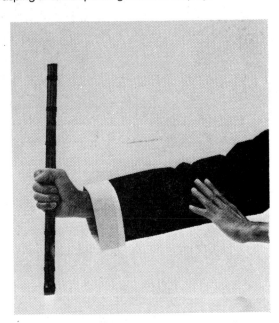

a. Strike down on your opponent's head with the end of the flute.

17

b. Strike to your opponent's nose or frontal region.

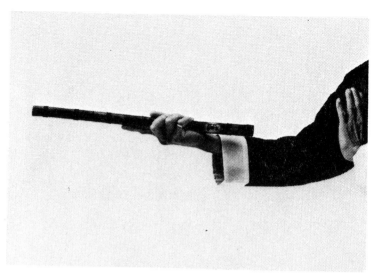

a. Strike poke with the end of the flute.

b. Stab with the end of the flute.

The Martial Potential of The Fatal Flute

The following techniques are the essential movements of the fatal flute form: 1) *dim*, "touch point"; 2) *hurn*, "circular"; 3) *chung*, "jam"; 4) *lan*, "block"; 5) *jeet*, "interception"; 6) *pou*, "parry"; 7) *tzu*, "stab."

1. *Dim*, "touch point"

2. *Hurn*, "circular"

3. *Chung*, "jam"

20

4. *Lan*, ''block''

5. *Jeet*, ''interception''

21

6. *Pou*, "parry"

7. *Tzu*, "stab"

2.
The Fatal Flute Form

"Form" is the term used for a set of movements put together in a sequence. Each movement is an individual technique for attack or self-defense. In the form, the movements follow in sequence, i.e., a defensive movement is followed by an attacking movement, then defense, then attack, etc. Each form has different techniques and applications, and varies in the degree of difficulty as the practitioner advances in the art of kung fu. Speed, anticipation, courage, confidence, power, a clear mind, and a strong healthy body, combined with technique will equip the martial artist for effective self-defense. In practicing the basic exercises and the form, you will gain most of the above attributes, but diligence and determination on your part are the prerequisites for success.

A brief description of the overall pattern of the fatal flute form may help you more easily understand the technique-by-technique breakdown of the form which is to follow. For the sake of convenience, it will be assumed that the practitioner begins facing east. The fatal flute form first moves north in a straight line from the point of origin. This is termed line A. Line B commences with a 180 degree turn bringing the student south down the performance line toward the starting point. Line C begins with a 180 degree turn along the performance line to the north. Line D is a final 180 degree turn which brings the practitioner south down the performance line to end precisely at the point of origin.

It should be understood that the wah lum style is characterized by fluidity and power. The stop-action photographs used here merely show major structure in what must be performed as an almost continuous flow of defense/attack techniques.

1. Begin line A, a northward line from the point of origin. Start ready position facing east.

2. Turn your face north (the body still facing east). The flute is raised to the right shoulder with an opened right hand. The right foot crosses over in front of the left foot to form a lady horse stance.

3. The body now shifts so that it is facing north, and the flute is formally presented in a traditional salutation. The left foot steps forward into a cat stance.

4. The left foot now retreats until you are standing in an erect position, with the right fist held at the right hip.

5. Bend the knees. The flute is now grasped in both hands in a transitional movement (slight pause).

6. The right foot steps forward to form a lady horse stance. The flute is shifted to the right hand. The body is now turned to the east in order to cut down on the target area. The flute is in position for a strong circular strike coming from behind the body.

7. The left hand is lowered into an on-guard position.

8. The body alone has shifted to face the west. The flute is brought down and across in a diagonal blocking movement. Note: the left arm adds support to the blocking arm. The body is still kept sideways to limit the exposed areas. The stance has become a cat stance with the right foot forward (no step was made).

9. The right foot lunges forward into a hill climbing stance. The tip of the flute is thrust forward while the left hand performs an upward block to protect the head.

10. The right foot is retracted while the flute is brought down in a circular block (a left to right clockwise circle). Note the shape of left hand.

11. Strike to the side of the head using the top end of the flute. The left hand guards while the right leg has advanced into a hill climbing stance.

12a, b, c. Take a short shuffle step forward (the feet are in the same relative position). The flute is maneuvered vertically for a strike to the head in a clockwise circle.

12b.

12c. (Side view of 12b.)

13. No step is involved as you twist the body to the east. The legs will automatically form a lady horse stance. The flute is held high to defend and prepare for attack.

14. Step forward with your left leg. Grab with the left hand, and prepare for a downward strike with the top end of the flute.

15. The right hand delivers a downward looping strike with the end of the flute. The target area is the top of the head.

16. Launch a right thrust kick to the head region.

17. After the kick, the right foot steps forward. Next, the left foot crosses behind it in a low lady horse stance while the right hand delivers an upward strike to the groin. The left hand protects the head.

18a and b. Perform a 360 degree counterclockwise turn. The left hand performs a scooping block and ends in a guard position over the head, while the right hand strikes the groin area with the flute.

19. Begin line B (a southward line) by dropping for a side thrust kick. You are now facing south.

20. A front view of the kick shown in 19.

21a. Rising from floor, still facing south, the practitioner places his right foot north of the left knee.

37

21b. Spinning to the left in a 180 degree arch, the performer stands performing grab with left hand and block with right hand flute . . .

21c. And strikes with the end of flute to the temple area.

22. Step forward with your right foot into a lady horse stance. The right hand performs a warding-off motion while the left hand guards with the flute over the head and prepares to strike.

23a and b. The striking sequence is the same as described in pictures #12a and b, except in this instance a cat stance is assumed.

24. Without changing your stance, perform a cross block to protect the upper torso. Note the position of flute, hand, and fingers.

25. Your hands separate and your left leg raises in preparation for a kick. Note the position of hands, left knee and right foot.

26. Launch a left thrusting kick to the upper region.

27. As you complete the sequence, the left foot steps forward into a hill climbing stance.

28. Without changing your foot position, turn your body to the west. The left hand grabs, while with the right hand the flute blocks to the rear and prepares to strike.

29. Begin the downward strike with the top of the flute. As the strike descends, describing a clockwise circle along the left side of the body, step forward with the right foot.

30. In a smooth continuous motion, step forward with the left foot, placing it behind the right foot assuming a low lady horse stance. The strike is made in a downward motion with the bottom end of the flute, while the left hand assumes a guard position over the head.

31a. Perform a 360 degree counterclockwise turn. The left hand forms a scooping block.

31b. End in a hill climbing stance with a right hand strike to the temple region with the top of the flute. The left hand supports the right and blocks in front of the performer's head.

32a. Step forward with the right foot. Maneuver the flute vertically in a clockwise circular strike to the head area.

32b. At the moment of the head strike, the performer is in a cat stance with his right foot forward.

33. Dropping more deeply into a cat stance, block to the left. Note the position of the left hand.

34. Step forward with your right foot into a hill climbing stance. Stab with the top of the flute, while executing an overhead guard with the left hand.

35a. Begin Line C, a northward movement. Make a 180 degree counterclockwise turn, left hand performing with the scooping block.

35b. End with a right overhead strike with the top of the flute. The left hand supports the right hand and the left foot is forward in a hill climbing stance.

47

36. Using the right hand for floor support, perform a low sweep with the right leg.

37. Continue the sweeping techniques with the left leg. Again, the hands are used on the side of the body opposite of the sweeping leg for floor support.

38. Your body weight moves forward from the right leg to left into a kneeling posture. The left arm is brought up into an overhead block, while a right jab is performed with the top end of the flute.

39. Advance with your right foot into a cat stance. Perform a circular parry to the right.

40. Drop to the left knee. The right hand blocks over the head region. The left hand attacks the groin.

41a. Begin line D, a southward line. Make a 180° counterclockwise turn. The left hand performs a scooping block.

41b. End in a hill climbing stance with the left foot forward. The left hand blocks over the head, the right hand strikes the chin area with top of the flute.

42. Advance with the right foot into a cat stance. Perform a circular parry to the right.

43. Dropping more deeply into a cat stance, block to the left.

43a. Step out with your right foot into a hill climbing stance and perform a circular strike with bottom end of the flute. This circular strike moves to the left of the performer as he looks down the performance line. Advance with the right foot and slide the left foot into a parallel position to repeat the circular strike once again.

43b. On the third circular strike, step in front of the right foot with the left into a low lady horse stance. The three circular downward strikes should be down in a rapid continuous motion.

44. Unwind to the left while leaning to the south in a cat stance, and strike over the left shoulder with the top end of flute. Both hands hold the flute, with the left below the right.

45. Step back with the right foot, then with the left foot and strike over the right shoulder. Lean in the direction of the strike.

46. Unwind 180 degree to the left and step into a cat stance with the right foot. Cross arms in a block to protect the upper torso.

47. Change the flute to the left hand, and perform a downward block while the right hand moves behind the head into a defensive posture. The body twists clockwise into a lady horse stance.

48. The left foot advances into a cat stance. Begin the finishing salute.

49. The left foot retreats into a cat stance. The right hand forms a fist.

50. Without changing foot position, withdraw the right fist to the hip, and the left hand with the flute to the hip.

51. The right foot moves back next to the left foot. The flute points toward the floor, with the right fist at the hip.

52. Close of the fatal flute form.

3.
Combat Applications of The Fatal Flute Form

In China, the kung fu artists used to say, "When the flute comes out as a weapon, someone is going to die." Almost every technique with the flute can kill. Short weapons, like the flute, fan, etc., do not appear to be dangerous to the untrained eye; but in fact, they might be more dangerous than longer weapons. It is said that with the flute, there is much danger in the movement of one inch.

It should be understood, however, that the techniques of the flute are very advanced. The flute is deadly only when used by a highly trained master who possesses the necessary internal power (*chi*), speed, flexibility, and control. The flute is, after all, only a short stick. The technique is in the practitioner, not the flute. Further, the force of the flute's blows to striking areas does not need to be fatal. With the precision stemming from long and earnest practice, the true and compassionate martial artist will first seek to warn a would-be attacker with lightly focused blows to striking areas. A wounding attack would only be used if the assailant continues the assault in spite of the warning.

The following series of photographs show a few self-defense techniques taken directly from the fatal flute form.

1. A block from the form.

2. Side view of the block.

3. Application of the blocking technique depicted in #1 and #2. The attacker delivers a right middle punch. Chan (right) parries the attacking arm . . .

4. and continues to strike the attacker under the chin.

5. A response to a right punch to the face. Note the grasping position of the right hand on the flute, and precise striking area.

6. A low blocking position from the form.

7. An application of the technique against a low side-kick.

8. A low blocking posture applied against a lower level staff attack.

63

9. Defense against an overhead staff attack. Note the use of the flute as a "hard ridge" to protect the arm and guide the power of the staff in a neutral direction.

10. A pressing block from a low cat stance, part of the fatal flute form.

11. The pressing block can be applied against a middle level thrust by a staff.

12. After blocking the staff, Chan steps forward with his right foot, striking with the front end of the flute.

13. In a variation of #12, the strike is delivered with the back end of the flute.

14. Chan blocks a high level strike by the staff (left hand forward).

15. Chan does not change position from #14 and responds to a high level strike by the staff (right hand forward).

16. When attacked by a knife, Chan moves outside the line of the attack, parries with the left hand and strikes the sensitive elbow area with the top of the flute. If delivered with power, the strike will break the elbow; with less power, it will cause temporary numbing of the left arm.

17. The attacker thrusts his staff toward the face area. Chan drops to his right knee, deflects the staff with his left hand, and strikes toward the armpit of the attacker with the right hand (front-end of the flute).

Striking with the Flute

The following photographs illustrate some, though not all, of the striking points vulnerable to the flute. Note the simultaneous attack/defense characteristics of the following techniques.

1. The strike into the armpit can kill.

2. The rib strike can cause severe pain and long-term internal damage.

3. Striking into this area of the back can paralyze the legs.

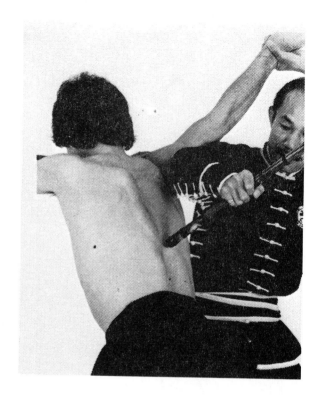

4. This target will cause lower body paralysis.

5. An attacking technique from the form.

6. Application of the technique. This attack can cause death.

7. A striking technique from the form.

8. Application of the technique — a killing strike.

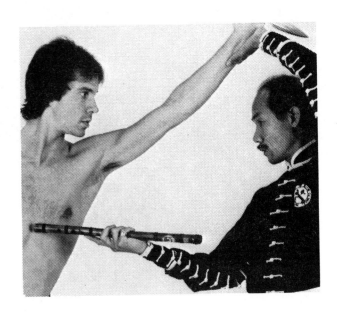

9. An overhead strike from the form.

10. Application of the technique — a killing strike.

11. A blow to the temples from the form.

74

12. Its application is a killing
strike.

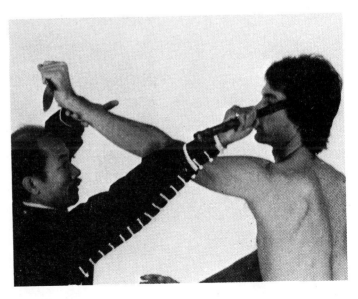

13. A strike to the head from the form.

14. Its application is another killing strike.

15. This attack will paralyze the neck region.

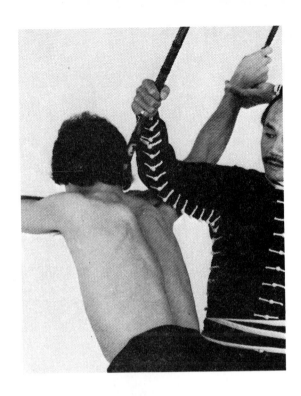

16. This blow to the throat is a killing strike.

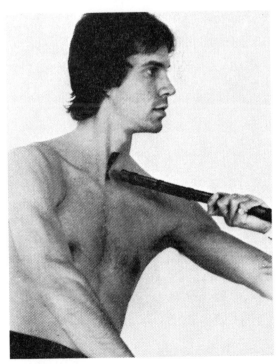

17. This attack will cause paralysis.

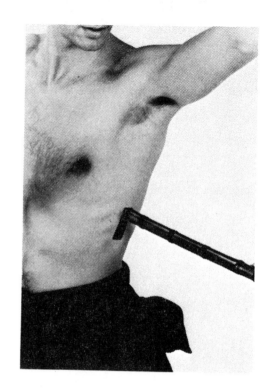

18. A killing strike.

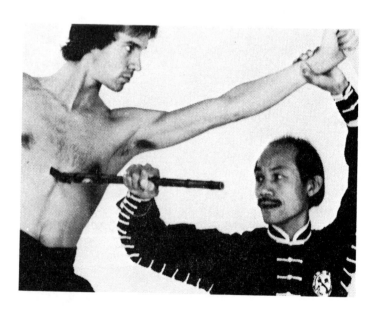

Wu Cheung. One of the heroes of *Water Margin*.

4.
The Fighting Stick

The Fighting Stick
in Chinese Culture

One of the unique characteristics of primates (monkeys, apes and humans) is their ability to grasp sticks for use as tools and weapons. This is due to the power grip (holding a hammer) and precision grip (holding a writing pen) capabilities of the primate hand. Non-human primates have been observed using sticks as projectiles and bludgeons, but rarely as a jabbing instrument. It is with the development of human culture that the spearing or stabbing use of the stick came into being, and it is from the spear that the movements of the kung fu fighting stick evolved.

A long pointed stick, employed as a javelin, lance, or spear, is an almost universal human weapon. Its use in China, as elsewhere, extends to the earliest periods of Chinese history. However, for the sake of tracing a specifically martial arts-oriented history of the long stick, we can begin with the Golden Age of Buddhism in China beginning about 265 A.D. The Shaolin Temple, for example, was built during the Chin Dynasty in 377 A.D. under Emperor Wei. During the succeeding Tang Dynasty (618-906 A.D.), the skill and artistry of the stick fighting techniques of the Shaolin monks became increasingly known as they employed this weapon to defend themselves against bandits — and also against official representatives of the state. The monks used the staff, instead of the spear, due to the Buddhist aversion to bloodshed and killing. The Tang was a turbulent period. It marked the rise of a professional army and the official proscription of Buddhism (868 A.D.).

A number of drawings have been preserved which show techniques from a Shaolin stick form whose theme is "Fighting in Darkness."

Many significant individuals are associated with the stick during the Sung Dynasty (960-1279). Lo Jin Yee, the second of the major characters in the literary classic *Water Margin* (*All Men Are Brothers*) was a great exponent of the fighting staff.

Fighting Stick Stances

1. Hill-climbing stance — on-guard position.

2. Lady-horse stance — on-guard position.

3. Left-handed stick. The left foot is always in front.

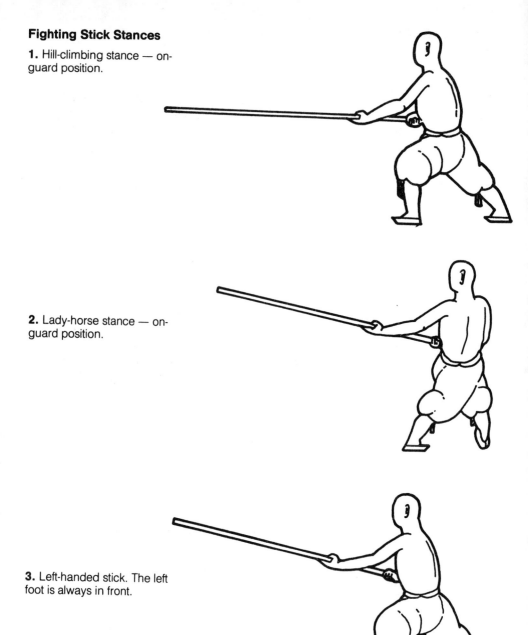

1. From a hill-climbing stance, on-guard position, move to . . .

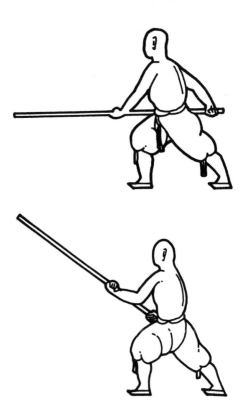

2. An outside circle block to the left. This is used to defend against an attack to the left side of the head.

1-2. Axe opening the mountain.

3. Fisherman throws the net.

1 & 2. Reverse to right hand technique.

1a. Return — left side.

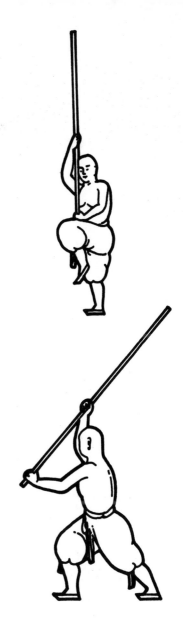

1b. Attack — power is in the front hand.

2a. Return — right side.

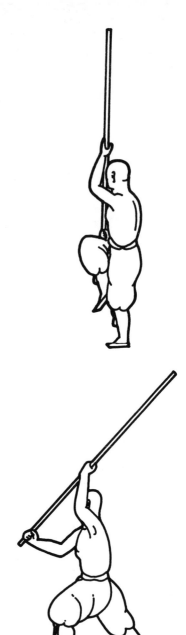

2b. Attack — power is in the front hand.

3. Circle Sticking technique.

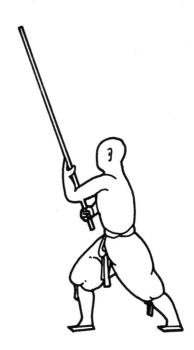

Likewise, the Sung period's King Chu was reputed to have excellent stick technique, and the family of General Yung became famous for its stick and spear methods.

The Ming Dynasty (begin 1368) witnessed the pinnacle of fame for the fighting arts of the Shaolin Temple. This high point of excellence was, perhaps, spurred by the incessant conflict between the Chinese patriots and the Manchus (Ching Dynasty) which lasted into the early twentieth century. One of those who fought against the Manchus was Ching Yeung. He had learned stick techniques from a Shaolin monk. When his side lost in their attempts to expel the Manchus, he shaved his head and became a monk of the Wah Lum Monastery in Shantung. As was mentioned earlier, Ching Yeung passed the style on to Lee Kwan Shan, who passed it on to the author, Sifu Chan Poi.

Aside from the historical perspective just outlined, some general comments about the stick in wah lum kung fu are appropriate at this point. The stick as a weapon is most associated with the south of China, while the spear is more associated with the north; however, the strategy and philosophy of the use of both weapons is the same. It is also said that the stick is like a grandfather, in that it has so many descendants. Many martial arts make the stick the first and last weapon taught. In addition, old people are expert users of the stick. Young martial artists may have greater explosive strength and stronger punching and kicking abilities, but it is with the elder martial artist that one finds the most devastating, effective, and subtle stick techniques.

The development of good stick technique is dependent upon developing the finger's strength for gripping and upon flexibility in the shoulders. The exercises described for use with the fatal flute form would be helpful to this end. It is also important to remember that the back hand, normally the left, should grip tightly and near the bottom of the stick, while the right hand grips more loosely to facilitate the sliding and twisting of the weapon. Notice the hand positions in the drawings of Shaolin stick techniques.

A final suggestion for the practice of the basic stick form is: "Keep yin and yang clearly distinguished." Be aware of the up and down, left and right, in and out, hard and soft aspects of the form. If you act with an awareness of this rule, your performance of the basic stick form will be more precise, more polished, and more powerful.

Stick techniques of General Chek of the Ming Dynasty.

1a. Opening your opponent for an attack with a high block.

1b. Opening your opponent for an attack with a low block.

2a. Low poke or ''sting'' to the opponent

2b. Shift your block to the side, then move in and attack.

89

a. "Eyebrow stick" technique — poke to the opponent's eyebrows.

b. "Water drip down" technique — strike to the knees.

c. High block and attack.

90

d. Middle block and strike technique.

e. High strike and block technique.

f. Low block and strike technique.

91

g. Opponents exchange strikes.

The Martial Potential
of the Fighting Staff

The following techniques are the essential movements of the wah lum basic stick form: 1) barring; 2) side block; 3) spiral thrust; 4) circular reaping block; 5) straight sliding thrust; 6) striking down; 7) high parry; 8) upward throat thrust; 9) upward flick.

1. Barring. A linear hard blocking technique.

2. Side Block. It is generally performed with a vigorous sweeping motion across the front of the body while the stick is held in a vertical position.

3. Spiral Thrust. At the point of contact the right hand performs a quick counter-clockwise turn giving the strike ("sting") a spiraling motion as it makes contact on the striking surface.

94

4. Circular reaping. It is a strong vertical circle performed in front of the body with the top end of the staff.

5. Straight sliding thrust. The sliding of the stick and the resultant hand positions distinguish this technique. As with all stings, a spiral is added to the impact with, in this instance, the back hand.

6. Striking. This is a vertical descending strike.

7. This is a circular deflecting block.

8. Upward throat thrust. Generally one advances strongly into this technique to give the stick power.

9. Upward flick. This is most obviously interpreted as a strike to the groin. However, as with all basic techniques, the possibilities are endless. In ancient times the upward flick maneuver might have been used to toss dirt in an attacker's eyes.

5.
The Basic Stick Form

For the sake of clarity, it will be assumed that the wah lum basic stick form begins with the practitioner facing east. The form moves from the point of origin on a straight line north (Line A), turns to the south (Line B), turns again to the north (Line C), and then returns to the starting point.

From the beginning of kung fu, short songs and poems have been associated with various techniques as memory aides for students. The brief statements usually depict an image or allusion that helps the student understand the basic body movement, feeling, or historical relationships of certain martial techniques. At central points, in the description to follow, pertinent fragments of these traditional poems will be presented in quotation marks under the picture of the technique which they describe.

1. Begin line A, a northward line. Assume the starting position, with the practitioner facing east.

2. Turn to the north and crouch. Grasp the stick with the left hand at the bottom.

3. Step north with the left foot. *"Little ghost holds the flag."*

4a. Perform a sweeping block to the left while holding the stick in a vertical position by shifting your weight toward the left foot.

4b. As hill climbing stance is formed, pass the stick across the front of the body from right to left. Note that the lower part of the stick must block below knee level. *"Open the window and look at the moon."*

5. Execute a downward strike. *"Laying down boards to make a dock."*

6a and b. Perform a left-to-right sweeping block by raising the left hand and passing the vertical stick vigorously in an arch to the right. "*Looking for a snake in tall grass.*"

7a. Step forward in a horse riding stance with body facing west while your gaze is to the north.

7b. Then strike down to knee level. "*Sit on the horse and attack*."

8a. Advance with the left foot into the lady horse stance.

8b. Then slide the stick through the right hand. Bring the left hand to meet it at the end of stick as the thrust to the upper body is performed. *"Poison snake comes out of its hole."*

9. Technique #8b observed from the side.

10. Step back with the left foot into a riding horse stance and strike down.

11. Raise your body and perform a high parry to the right by moving the stick in a horizontal counterclockwise arch. *"Part clouds and look at the sun."*

12a. Slide right hand to end of stick.

12b. Perform an overhead downward strike to the northeast.

13. Execute a high parry to the left. The stick is moved in a horizontal counterclockwise arch.

14a. Slide the left hand to the end of the stick and step with the left foot into the hill climbing stance.

14b. Perform spiral thrust to the head region. The strike is to the northwest. *"Central striking."*

15. Perform a circular block by reaping with the stick in a clockwise circle.

16. Step with the right foot into the hill climbing stance and perform a high parry to the right.

17. Step through with the left foot into a low lady horse stance and strike to the northeast.

17a. Pictures 17a-d show a double 360 degree cut. Move the left hand under the right arm, and turn the right hand over in preparation for a 360 degree counterclockwise body turn.

111

17b. Unwinds to the left with the right hand down and the left hand up performing a low sweeping block around body.

17c. As the body continues to turn toward the north, the left leg is raised while the stick describes another 360 degree overhead cut, to untangle the arms.

17d. End in this position.
"Tornado stick technique."

18a. Jump onto the left foot.

18b. Quickly continue to step forward with the right foot into the hill climbing stance while striking toward the head region.

19. Rock back onto the left lef and block to the north. "*Turn body and gaze at the moon.*"

20a. Begin line B, a southward line. Perform a 180 degree counterclockwise turn to the south, while feet remain stationary.

20b. Block to the left side.

20c. And strike down.

21a and b. Perform a block across the front of the body while the feet remain positioned.

22a. Step forward with the right foot into the horse riding stance. The body faces east, your gaze is to the south.

22b. Strike down to knee level.

23a. Advance with the left foot into the lady horse stance.

23b. Slide the stick through the right hand. Bring the left hand to meet it at the end of the stick as the thrust to the upper body is performed.

24a. Step back with the left foot into the horse riding stance and strike down.

24b. Execute a high parry to the right. The feet remain stationary.

25a. Slide your right hand to the end of the stick.

25b. Perform a downward strike to the southwest.

26. Execute a high parry to the left. Your stick moves in a horizontal counterclockwise arch.

27a. Slide your left hand to the end of the stick, and step with the left foot into a hill climbing stance.

27b. Perform a spiral thrust to the southeast.

28. Perform a circular block by reaping with the stick in a clockwise vertical circle.

29. Step with the right foot into the hill climbing stance and perform a high parry to the right.

30. Step through with the left foot into a low lady horse stance and strike to the southwest.

31a. Pictures 17a-d show a double 360 degree cut. Move the left hand under the right arm, and turn the right hand over in preparation for a 360 degree counterclockwise body turn.

124

31b. Unwinds to the left with the right hand down and the left hand up performing a low sweeping block around body.

31c. As the body continues to turn toward the north, the left leg is raised while the stick describes another 360 degree overhead cut, to untangle the arms.

31d. End in this position. "*Tornado stick technique.*"

31e. Jump onto the left foot. Quickly continue to step forward with the right foot into the hill climbing stance while striking toward the head region.

126

32. Stepping forward on the right foot, assume the hill climbing stance and perform a spiral strike to the head region.

33. Rock back onto the left leg and block to the south.

34. Begin line C, a northward line. turn 180 degree in a counterclockwise motion and strike to the foot area. *"Chicken pecking for rice."*

35. Lift the left foot, and perform a vertical block to the right.

36. Jump to the left foot and then step out with the right foot into a cat stance while striking to the foot area.

37. Proceed into this technique with a stagger step. From the previous position, step out with the right foot, step with the left foot, and step again with the right foot. Drop into a right foot forward, low crouch and strike to the throat backing the staff with the floor. *"Placing incense, locking the throat."*

38. Step out with the right foot into a cat stance, and perform an upper level block. "*Raising the ridgepole.*"

39. Raising the right hand and lowering the left, perform a block across the upper and middle body area.

40. Without changing your foot position, strike down with the right end of the stick.

41. Employ a large clockwise circular reap to the left side while the right foot is lifted. End in a high parry to the right.

42a. Step back with the right foot into a hill climbing stance. At the same time, make a large low circular reap across the front of the body.

42b. End with a second smaller reaping block as the stick points to the northwest.

43. Turn to the northeast. Raise up on the right heel. Point the top of the stick to the floor and block across the body with the stick in a vertical position.

44. Step to the east into a low cat stance while looking to the north. Revolve the stick from the top-down position in which it was taken at the end of the sweeping block to the right, and into a vertical top-up position in a counterclockwise arch. The cat stance and the final stick position should be assumed simultaneously.

45. Step back with the left, and draw the right foot back to a matching position. At the same time, the left hand moves in a large counter-clockwise circle on the left side of the body. The performer rises to a standing position as he positions the left hand at his side in the final position.

46. The final position, facing the east.

6.
Combat Applications of The Fighting Stick

The following photographs depict defense/attack exercises drawn from the wah lum basic stick form. The form, of course, holds many more practice combinations than will be presented. It may also be interesting to compare the wah lum stick techniques with those depicted earlier in the drawings of the Shaolin and Ming era stick practitioners.

1a. Block and Attack. Attack with the side strike to the left side of your opponent's head. Defend with a vertical block to the left. At the same time, lean back, away from the strike.

1b. Both opponents attack simultaneously to the head.

1a. Block and Attack. From a riding horse stance, attack with a poke to your opponent's midsection. Defend with a vertical block from a cat horse stance.

2b. Attack with a poke to the midsection from a riding horse stance. Defend and attack simultaneously by blocking with the left hand and striking the opponent's head with your right hand.

3a. Block and Attack. Attack
with a poke to the midsection
from a riding horse stance.
Defend with a vertical block
from a cat horse stance.

3b. Attack with a poke to the
midsection. Block with the left
hand, while striking to the side
of the opponent's knee with
the right hand.

4a. Attack with a poke to the midsection from a hill climbing stance. Defend by stepping at a 15 degree angle to the side, and striking down on the opponent's lead hand.

4b. Simultaneously attack the head and the side of the knee.

141

5a. Attack to the head from a hill climbing stance. Defend with a small circle of the wrist to the outside from a cat horse stance.

5b. Simultaneous Attacks. Poke to the midsection from the hill climbing stance. Then strike the back of the neck from the same stance.

6a. Attack and Defend.
Attack with a strike to the opponent's head from a hill climbing stance. Defend with a small circle of the wrist to the outside from a cat horse stance.

6b. Simultaneous attacks to the head.

7a. Block and Attack. Attack
with a flick up to the groin
from a hill climbing stance.
Defend with a horizontal block
from the same stance.

7b. Attack and Defend.
Attack your opponent's head
from a hill climbing stance.
Defend and attack
simultaneously by dropping
down into a half-butterfly
stance and poking up to the
throat or chin.

144

8a. Attack and Defend.
Attack with a poke to the knee from a riding horse stance. Defend with an inside block close to the opponent's leg.

8b. Attack and Defend.
Attack with a strike to the knee from a low riding horse stance. Defend by blocking down on the opponent's stick from the same stance.

9a. Attack and Defend.
Attack with an overhead strike from a hill climbing stance. Defend with a high horizontal block from a cat horse stance.

9b. Attack and Defend.
Attack with a low strike to the side of your opponent's knee from a hill climbing stance. Defend with a vertical block to the outside from a cat horse stance.

Appendix:
Basic Stances

The following three stances are used frequently in both the fatal flute and basic stick forms.

1. Cat Stance

The leading foot will hold 10 percent of your body weight. Your back foot will support 90 percent of your body weight. The leading foot is touching the ground only with the toe

2. Hill Climbing Stance

From the riding horse position, twist your waist to your left. Your upper torso should face completely to the side. Your feet must still be in the same position. The back leg must be straight. Weight distribution: 60 percent leading leg, 40 percent back leg.

3. Lady Horse Stance

This stance derives its name from the character "lady" in Chinese. When you cross your right leg in front of your left, your leg will resemble that character. Eyes remain in the direction of the opponent. Weight distribution: 70 percent leading leg, 30 percent back leg.

Unique Publications Book List

Unique Publications, Inc.
4201 Vanowen Place
Burbank, California 91505

Please write or call for our latest catalog.

(800) 332-3330